BENJAMIN ADLARD COUNTY SCHOOL
SANDSFIELD LANE
GAINSBOROUGH. DN21 1DB

2683   301·3

LOOK AROUND THE STREET

Clive Pace and Jean Birch

Illustrated by Steve Wheele

How to use this book

Use this book to help you discover things about the streets around your home and school. Try to find out as much as you can. The answers to some of the questions are at the back of the book, but don't look at them until you have tried to work them out for yourself. Some of the questions only you can answer because they are about the area you live in.

Never leave your home or school without first telling an adult where you are going. When you are walking around in the street remember to be very careful. Stay on the pavement and never cross the road without help from an adult. Never talk to strangers.

Look Around You

Look Around Homes
Look Around the Park
Look Around the School
Look Around Shops
Look Around the Street
Look Around Transport

Editor: Jannet King/Marcella Streets
Designer: Ross George

First published in 1988 by
Wayland (Publishers) Ltd
61 Western Road, Hove
East Sussex, BN3 1JD, England

© Copyright 1988 Wayland (Publishers) Ltd

British Library Cataloguing in Publication Data
Pace, Clive
 The Street
 1. Streets. — For children.
 I. Title. II. Birch, Jean. III. Series
 388.1

ISBN 1 85210 468 6

Phototypeset by Kalligraphics Ltd, Horley, Surrey
Printed and bound in Belgium by Casterman S.A.

Contents

How to use this book	**6**
Street names	**8**
The pavement	**10**
Post boxes	**12**
Telephone boxes	**14**
Machines in the street	**16**
Lights in the street	**18**
At work in the street	**20**
Markings and signs	**22**
Barriers and bollards	**24**
The past in your street	**26**
What did you find out?	**28**
Glossary	**29**
Further reading	**30**
Index	**30**

Answers to questions are on page 28.
All the words that are underlined appear
in the glossary on page 29.

STREET NAMES

Streets are often named after a building in them.

Can you guess what this street is called?

Can you find other streets named after buildings?

Some streets are named after the people who used to work there.

▲
**What work did the people who worked in these streets do?
What other streets are named after people's jobs?**

8

Streets are often named after famous people.
Can you find out who these people were?

Some streets record famous events.
What kind of events were these?

Some streets are named after rivers or trees.
Can you find some interesting street names near you?

THE PAVEMENT

Look at the pavement outside your school.

**What is it made of?
Is it like the one outside your house?**

▲
Some pavements are made of paving stones.

▲
Most pavements these days are made of tarmac.

Do you know what tarmac is?

Some shopping centres have large paved areas. These can be made to look attractive, with bricks, paving stones and even cobblestones arranged in patterns.

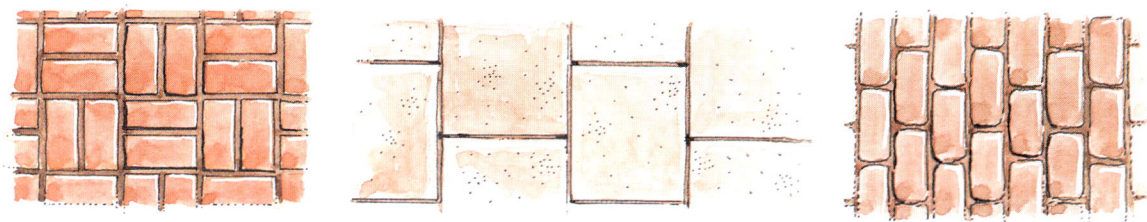

Find some interesting patterns in the street and copy them on a piece of paper.

Look closely at the pavement as you walk along. Outside houses you will find metal covers like these.
What do you think is under them?

How many different kinds of cover can you find on the pavement?
Can you draw some of them?

POST BOXES

**Is there a post box near your house?
What shape is it?**

It might be round and stand on the pavement.
▼

Or it might be rectangular and set in a wall.
▼

**Have you seen other types of post box?
Why do you think post boxes are red?**

When is the post box near you emptied?

Look at the information panel on it. This tells you the times when letters are collected. The 'next collection' number at the top tells you when the postman or postwoman will be back.

Go to the post box with a parent when the postman or postwoman is due. Ask if the number of letters is different at each collection.

Every post box has <u>initials</u> like these on it.

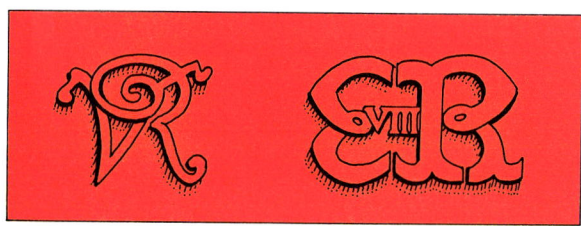

▲
Do you know what these initials mean? How many different initials can you find?

TELEPHONE BOXES

Is there a telephone box near your home? What does it look like?

▲ Old telephone boxes are red with a door and clear glass windows.

▲ Many modern telephone boxes have large panes of grey glass.

Why do you think the shape and colour of telephone boxes have changed?

Have you ever used a telephone box?

They can sometimes be difficult to spot because there are different types and many are no longer red.

▲ Some have no door.   ▲ Some have just a hood.

One day you may need to telephone for the police, for the fire brigade or for an ambulance.
Do you know how to make an emergency call?

MACHINES IN THE STREET

Have you noticed all the machines in the street?

You may well have used machines like this.

▲
You may have seen one of these machines outside a bank or a building society.

What is it for?

Have you ever seen one of these machines?
▼

It gives tourists all kinds of information. To use it you touch the numbered buttons with your finger. The computer then shows you what you want to know.

If you were visiting a new town, what kinds of things would you want to know?

What is this machine for? ▶

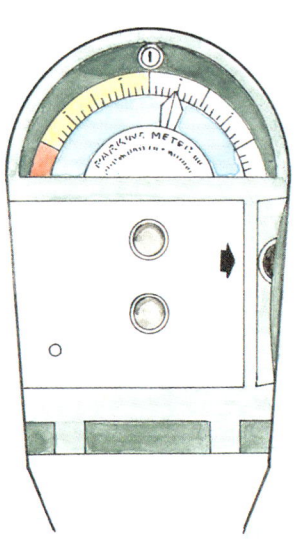

You put money into a slot in the side and the pointer moves across the dial.

There is still some time left to run on this machine.

17

LIGHTS IN THE STREET

Are there streetlamps outside your home? What shape are they?

▲ Some streetlamps have an orange light.

What colour are they when they first come on?

▲ Some old streetlamps are interesting shapes. See how many different kinds of streetlamp you can find.

Do you know what colours traffic lights are?

Do you know what the colours mean?

Flashing orange globes on zebra crossings warn drivers that people may be crossing.

▼

These globes are called Belisha beacons.
Do you know why?

AT WORK IN THE STREET

How many different people can you think of who work in the street?

Sometimes workers dig up the road. They may have to reach pipes which run under it. Or they may put a new surface on it.

◀ People who deliver milk drive milkfloats or vans.

If you have milk delivered to your home, do you know what time it arrives?

Have you ever seen a road sweeper?

◀ Some road sweepers use brushes.

Some use machines.

The driver of a street cleaning machine has to be very careful when driving along the pavement.
Why is this?

MARKINGS AND SIGNS

Have you ever noticed markings like these at road junctions? ▼

Who is meant to take notice of them?

Do you know what they mean?

Are there any double yellow lines painted in the gutter near your home? ▶

Do you know what they mean?

Can you find any other kinds of yellow markings on the road?

Try to find out what they mean.

Is there a sign like this near your school?
▼

It warns drivers to look out for children.

Can you work out what these signs mean?

Make up your own signs for 'men digging' and 'railway crossing'.

BARRIERS AND BOLLARDS

Why are there <u>barriers</u> on the side of the road in some places?
▼

Can you think of places near your home where there are barriers?

Do you know what these barriers pointing upwards are for?
▼

Bollards like these can be seen in the middle of the road.
Do you know what they are for?
▼

The arrow tells drivers to keep to the left of the bollard.

Are there any bollards near your home?

Some bollards are made of metal and can be laid flat on the ground to let cars go over them. If you see any posts like this, have a look for signs of a lock on them. ▶

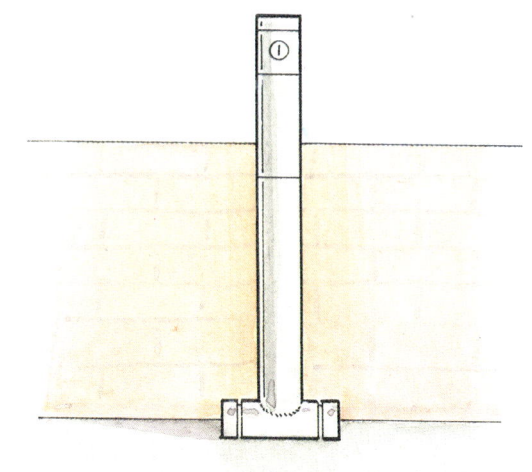

See how many different styles of bollard and barrier you can find.
What is each kind used for?

THE PAST IN YOUR STREET

Do you know what a war memorial is?

Is there one in your town or village?

This memorial reminds villagers of men who died in the First World War (1914–18). ▶

Look carefully at all the names on the memorial where you live. You may find that many members of the same family were killed in the same war.

Are any of your relatives remembered on a war memorial?

Famous people may have been born or may have stayed in your town.

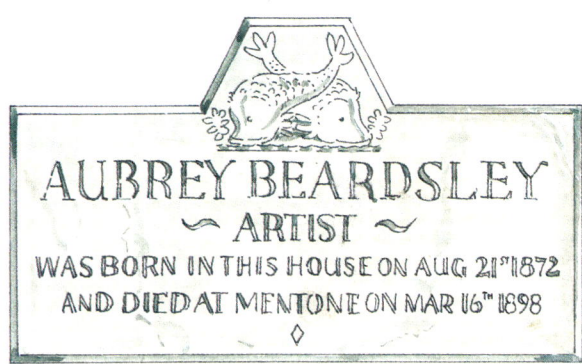

◀ **Are there any plaques like this to record the event?**

Can you find other signs of history in your street?
You might come across some of these.

What were they for?
Don't forget to keep your eyes open. The street is full of interesting things.

What did you find out?

Page 8:
The street is called Church Street.
A **baker** makes bread and cakes.
A **farrier** puts shoes on horses.

Page 9:
The Duke of **Wellington** (1769–1852) was commander of the British troops when they won the Battle of Waterloo. Later he was British Prime Minister.
Lord **Nelson** (1758–1805) was killed on his ship, HMS *Victory*, at the Battle of Trafalgar.
Queen **Victoria** (1819–1901) was Queen of Great Britain and Ireland for 64 years. She was the longest reigning British monarch.
Florence **Nightingale** (1820–1910) was famous for nursing wounded soldiers during the Crimean War.
The Battle of **Trafalgar** (1805) was a sea battle fought by the British fleet under Lord Nelson against the Spanish and French.
The Battle of **Waterloo** (1815) was fought by the British against the French army under Napoleon.
A **coronation** is the ceremony at which a king or queen is crowned.
A **jubilee** is a celebration of a special anniversary, usually 25 or 50 years. Queen Victoria celebrated her Diamond Jubilee in 1897 after she had been queen for 60 years. Queen Elizabeth II celebrated her Silver Jubilee in 1977 after she had been queen for 25 years.

Page 10:
Tarmac is made of crushed stone mixed with tar and bitumen. Its full name is tarmacadam and it was invented by John McAdam in the last century.

Page 12:
Post boxes are red so that people can see them easily.

Page 13:
The **initials** on the post box tell you which king or queen was reigning when it was made. Very old ones have VR on them, for Victoria Regina (which means Queen Victoria). A few have EVIII for Edward VIII, who was king for less than a year in 1936, though he was never crowned.

Page 14:
Modern **telephone boxes** are easier to keep clean. They have a gap at the bottom so that leaves and rubbish will blow away. The materials and design make them more difficult to damage. Some boxes have yellow paintwork to match the colour of the British Telecom vans.

Page 15:
To make an **emergency call**, lift the telephone receiver and dial 999. You do not need to put any money into a public phone box for this. When the operator answers, say whether you want the fire brigade, police or an ambulance. If you are not sure, just tell them what has happened. You will need to tell them the telephone number you are calling from and, most important, where you are and where the people are who need help. There is a sign in telephone boxes telling you the address of the box.

Page 16:
Cash dispensers outside banks and building societies will give you money out of your account if you have a special card. You have to type in your personal number. They will also tell you how much money you have in your account. With some machines you can pay money into your account.

Page 17:
The machine is a **parking meter**. Motorists parking their cars next to them put in money. The dial then shows how long they are allowed to leave their cars there. When the time has run out a traffic warden may come along and give them a parking ticket. This means that they have to pay a fine.

Page 18:
When the **streetlamps** first come on they are red.

Page 19:
Traffic lights are red at the top, amber (yellow) in the middle and green at the bottom. Red means stop. Green means go. Amber means get ready.
Belisha beacons are named after Leslie Hore-Belisha. He was Minister of Transport and introduced them in the 1930s.

Page 21:
Street cleaners driving machines on the pavement have to be careful to avoid people. Also they must not bump into street lamps or other objects on the pavement.

Page 22:
Yellow criss-cross markings at traffic lights are for motorists. Drivers are not allowed to stop on them because they would block traffic coming the other way.

Double yellow lines tell motorists that they should not park at that point.

Page 23:
No overtaking.
The road narrows ahead.
Children crossing.
Slippery road.

Page 24:
The **barriers** prevent people from crossing the road at a dangerous point.
The **barriers** pointing upwards come down across the road when a train is approaching.

Page 27:
A footscraper for taking mud off boots and shoes.
A horse trough for horses to drink from.
A drinking fountain.

Glossary

<u>Barrier</u>   Something which stops you from moving from one place to another.
<u>Bollard</u>   A short post.
<u>Cobblestones</u>   Round stones which used to be laid on the ground to make a firm road surface. These days they are normally used for decoration on pavements.
<u>Initial</u>   The first letter of a word.
<u>Plaque</u>   A flat piece of stone, metal or other material attached to a wall. It has information on it which usually tells you about something which happened in the past.

29

Further reading

Safety on the Road by Dorothy Baldwin and Clare Lister (Wayland, 1986)
Safety When Alone by Dorothy Baldwin and Clare Lister (Wayland, 1987)
A Day with a Dustman by Chris Fairclough (Wayland, 1984)
A Day with a Postman by Graham Rickard (Wayland, 1984)
A Day with a Milkman by Christa Stadtler (Wayland, 1984)

Picture acknowledgements

British Telecom: Telefocus 15 (left); Cephas 10 (left), 18 (left), 19 (top), 20 (right), 22 (left), 24 (bottom); Chris Fairclough 22 (bottom); C. L. Pace 10 (right), 12 (right), 15 (right), 16 (left and right), 17, 18 (right), 21 (bottom), 23, 24 (top); Sefton Photo Library 21 (top); Wayland Picture Library 20 (left); Tim Woodcock cover, 8, 12 (left), 14 (left and right), 19 (bottom), 26.

Index

Bank 16, 28–9
Barriers 24, 29
Belisha beacons 19, 29
Bollards 25, 29
Bricks 11
Building society 16, 28–9

Cobblestones 11, 29
Colours 12, 14, 18, 19, 28, 29

Emergency telephone call 15, 28

History 27, 29

Lights 18–19, 29
   traffic 19, 29

Machines 16–17, 20, 28, 29
Milk delivery 20

Names 8–9, 13, 28, 29

Parking meter 17, 29
Pavement 10–11
Paving stones 10
Plaques 27, 29
Post boxes 12–13, 28

Road junctions 22, 29
Road markings 22
Road signs 23, 29
Road sweepers 21

Shapes 12, 14, 18, 28
Streetlamps 18, 29

Tarmac 10, 28
Telephone boxes 14–15, 28
Tourist information 17

War memorial 26

Zebra crossings 19